Did You

GRIMSBY

A MISCELLANY

Compiled by Julia Skinner
With particular reference to the work of David Peasgood

THE FRANCIS FRITH COLLECTION

www.francisfrith.com

Based on a book first published in the United Kingdom in 2004 by The Francis Frith Collection®

Hardback edition published exclusively for Identity Books in 2011 ISBN 978-1-84589-401-6

Text and Design copyright The Francis Frith Collection®
Photographs copyright The Francis Frith Collection® except where indicated.

British Library Cataloguing in Publication Data

Did You Know? Grimsby - A Miscellany
Compiled by Julia Skinner
With particular reference to the work of David Peasgood

The Francis Frith Collection
Oakley Business Park, Wylye Road,
Dinton, Wiltshire SP3 5EU
Tel: +44 (0) 1722 716 376
Email: info@francisfrith.co.uk
www.francisfrith.com

Printed and bound in Malaysia

Front Cover: **GRIMSBY, THE ROYAL DOCK c1955** G60019p

The colour-tinting is for illustrative purposes only, and is not intended to be historically accurate

CONTENTS

INTRODUCTION

By the 1920s Grimsby had grown into the largest and most prosperous fishing port in the world. A huge tonnage of cod, haddock and herring from the North Sea and the Icelandic fishing grounds was processed in the town to supply the length and breadth of the nation. During the inter-war years there was exceptional growth of the steam trawler fleets based in both Hull and Grimsby. These ships, with their port registration letters 'H' for Hull and 'G' for Grimsby, are seen in many of the photographs of the docks at this time. It is an astonishing fact that Grimsby alone, from this time and until the mid 1970s, provided one fifth of all the fish consumed in the UK. The eventual decline in the industry came as a result of the fishing limitations that Iceland placed on its fishing ground, which resulted in the aptly named 'cod wars' of the 1970s. The outcome was a huge decline in fish landings and the eventual loss of the deep sea trawling fleet - the Grimsby fishing industry was decimated. Fortunately though, Grimsby people adapt. Smaller shallow-water seine fishermen took over, and with a substantial fresh fish processing and cold storage facility in town, fish was still brought overland to Grimsby for sale and processing. The overall difference in fish tonnages passing through Grimsby is much reduced, but it has not spelt a death knell for the docks.

In recent years the Grimsby and Cleethorpes region has become one of the big commercial success stories, and the area has enjoyed unprecedented levels of inward investment. For several consecutive years the massive twin ports of Grimsby and Immingham have been confirmed as the largest and busiest ports in the UK. Internationally they are the sixth busiest port complex in Europe, whilst Immingham alone is the second busiest ferry terminal in the country. Over 10% of the nation's foodstuffs passes through the ports each day. Grimsby

has set a standard as Europe's food capital, which keeps the docks especially alive and flourishing, and trade in Grimsby's £14 million state-of-the-art fish market is busy. Grimsby is now both the UK centre for buying, selling and freezing fish, and one of Europe's premier fishing and fish processing centres, with the largest frozen storage capacity in Europe.

Appropriately for a place with such a strong fishing tradition, the multi-award-winning National Fishing Heritage Centre opened at the Alexandra Dock at Grimsby in 1991. The trawler 'Ross Tiger', which is moored outside the centre, is an excellent reminder of the proud heritage that built the town.

GRIMSBY, ALEXANDRA DOCK 1904 51829

LINCOLNSHIRE WORDS AND PHRASES

'Yellowbelly' - a term for someone born and bred in Lincolnshire. There are many theories about the origin of the name, but one of the favourite explanations is that it derives from the bright yellow waistcoat which was worn by the 10th Regiment of Foot, later The Lincolnshire Regiment.

'Chunter' - to complain.

'Frim folk' - people from other area.

'Jiffle' - fidget.

'Kecks' - trousers.

'Kelch' - mud.

'Mardy' - bad tempered, sulky.

'Nunty' - old fashioned, outdated.

'Proggle' - to poke about (with a stick).

'Reasty' - rancid.

'Throng' - busy.

'Starnil' - a starling.

'Uneppen' - clumsy.

'Wassack' or 'Gump' - a fool.

'Wick' - lively.

'Yucker' - a young person.

On **'Mumping Day'** - or St Thomas's Day, 21st December - it was the custom in Lincolnshire for poor people to go around begging for Christmas fare.

It was an old Lincolnshire belief that when a baby was born with noticeably large ears, it was a sign that he or she would be successful in life.

HAUNTED GRIMSBY

The gatehouse of Thornton Abbey (see photograph 33275 on page 21) is said to be haunted by the ghost of Sir Thomas de Grethem, a 14th-century abbot. He was put on trial for witchcraft and lax living, and punished by being walled up alive in a secret chamber. In the 1830s workmen found his skeleton sitting at a desk, complete with papers, ink, and the manuscript of his tale, which reads thus: 'They told lies about me, They accused me of witchery and black magic. I was in love with Heloise, the beautiful daughter of Sir William Wellam. She was a student of mine, and she loved me too. I know it was wrong, but I did not deserve to die. They put me on trial for lax living and I was found guilty. My punishment was left up to the Dean; he was the one who made up the stories about me. They have walled me up alive in a secret chamber in the abbey'. He concluded: 'If you see me wandering round the ruins of the abbey late at night, do not be afraid; I just want to be with my love'.

One of Grimsby's oldest pubs, the Old Coach House, is said to be haunted by the ghost of a young boy who was killed in an accident in a barn there.

The old school in Eleanor Street, which was Grimsby Art School for a time, is said to be haunted by two ghosts. One is a child who died in a swimming accident, and the other is a teacher who died on the top floor of the building. The sound of him smacking his cane against his hand can still be heard at times!

In recent years, the building that currently houses Beagles Lighting in Cleethorpes Road has been the subject of a number of mysterious events reported by staff. These include light bulbs suddenly dropping from the ceiling, unexplained shadows, doors opening and slamming, the front door opening for no reason so that the alarm is set off, echoing footsteps, and boxes in the store room being disarranged at night. Paranormal investigators concluded that the building is haunted by the ghosts of an elderly woman and two men, one of whom comes over as very aggressive and may have killed his wife there.

GRIMSBY MISCELLANY

A carved stone bust of Gervase Holles, former mayor and Grimsby MP, can be seen on the outside of the Town Hall (see photograph G60706 below). This renowned historian became Mayor of Grimsby in 1640, and was a patriot and a Royalist, supporting Charles I during the Civil War. Many of his manuscripts were destroyed, but among those remaining is the Grimsby Magna, a fascinating history of medieval Grimsby.

GRIMSBY, CARVING OF GERVASE HOLLES 2004 G60706

A gullible Grimbarian seen walking down Freeman Street in 1590 with a live toad tied around his neck probably had the plague. The toad was thought to draw the supposed poison out.

Opposite the Wheatsheaf Inn (see photograph G60709 below) in around 1820 lived Tommy Wilkinson, an old Waterloo man. He was so thoroughly convinced that there was a gold mine beneath his garden that he began to dig; he excavated a massive hole over many years, though all to no avail.

GRIMSBY, THE WHEATSHEAF INN ON BARGATE 2004 G60709

The former Grimsby mayor and Member of Parliament Gervase Holles was convinced that a curse rested upon the desecration of St Mary's Church and the stones of the building. Unfortunately, his great-uncle Densel Holles, who lived at Irby, did not heed his great-nephew's advice. Densel planned to build a new house at Irby, and purchased 'bargain' stone from the old St Mary's Church, but before he could lay a single stone he dropped down literally stone dead!

Abbey Road was so named in the early 19th century; it was previously known as Love Lane and Watery Lane. It was called Watery Lane because it was often flooded. It was only twelve feet wide in some parts.

In the 1800s the original Vicarage House to St James's Church was a lovely thatched cottage called the Homestall, situated opposite an entrance to the churchyard. It is now long gone.

The penalty for evasion of toll duties for visitors to the town was rather severe - you were hung on Gallows Hill next to the Weelsby road turnpike.

GRIMSBY, PUBLIC LIBRARY 2004 G60714

GRIMSBY, THE AVENUE, THE PEOPLE'S PARK c1955 G60005

One tenth of all the nation's foodstuffs passes through the ports of Grimsby and Immingham every day.

Halfway down Bargate is the Wheatsheaf Public House. In Victorian days, the landlady for many years was Mary Plumtree. She was described as 'a very thin and precise person, whose gown skirts only contained three widths of a gown piece, and whose companion was a lark with a wooden leg.'

Drunks who were placed in the Brighowgate stocks often stayed that way, as well-meaning friends would bring them beer and tobacco to ease the standard sentence time of six hours.

William Sherlock, the son of the Governor of the Alfred Terrace workhouse, had a vicious way of curing what he called 'sham sick, idle and disorderly' inmates and staff. One of the matrons was found guilty of assaulting an inmate; she was tied to the treadmill and flogged with osiers and a tough stick 'until the parts flogged were black with diffused blood beneath her skin.'

GRIMSBY, FISH DOCKS c1965 G60081

From Grimsby it is possible to reach 75% of the United Kingdom within the space of a single day's journey.

Debtors placed in the Town Hall gaol were never fed - unless they paid for the food themselves!

The Aldermen of the last century, who were frequently contracted to undertake building work in the borough, fervently believed in the dignity of labour. To the least scrupulous, an aldermanic labourer was of superior quality to a non-aldermanic labourer. They tended to pay themselves, on average twice as much per day as the general workers.

The founder of modern Methodism, John Wesley, made several visits to Grimsby, preaching both at St James' and at the Dissenting Meeting House in the adjacent Bull Ring. In one visit he described Grimsby as being 'no bigger than a middling village, containing a small number of half-starved inhabitants'!

Internationally, the twin ports of Grimsby and Immingham make up the sixth busiest port complex in Europe, whilst Immingham alone is the second busiest ferry terminal in the country.

GRIMSBY, TOWN HALL 1890 26726

GRIMSBY, OLD MARKET PLACE
c1965 G60058

When the old Town Hall was demolished in 1780, the wood from the old building sold for £2 19s 10d, and the tiles sold for £1 10s 8d. The ten labourers who completed the entire demolition in just eight days earned 1s 4d a day, or just seven new pence in today's terms.

Each July, the ceremony of swan-upping takes place on the Thames. This tradition dates back to the 12th century, and was once performed all over the country. A census was taken of the unmarked mute swans on the river, which were then claimed for the crown. When the census was completed, a toast would be made to the monarch, and in Grimsby's Black Swan Inn the toast was: 'To His (or Her) Majesty the King (or Queen), Seigneur of the Swans'.

During the Second World War, there were 37 air raids on Grimsby, and locals had to use their Anderson air raid shelters at the bottom of their gardens sometimes two or three times a night. In total, 197 Grimsby residents were killed in raids, which often centred on the docks and spread to the high-density housing nearby.

A survey by business specialists Dun & Bradstreet in 2001 labelled Great Grimsby as Britain's boom town, with more companies making a profit here than anywhere else in the country. The survey, based on the country's biggest 50,000 businesses in 150 towns and cities, found that 88.5 per cent of the town's major firms made a profit in the year 2000.

GRIMSBY, THE ROYAL DOCK c1955 G60019

GRIMSBY, THE OLD MARKET PLACE c1965 G60082

GRIMSBY, ALBERT STATUE 1890 26728

The Grimsby and Cleethorpes region has become one of the commercial success stories of recent years, enjoying unprecedented levels of inward investment. For the fourth consecutive year the massive twin ports of Grimsby and Immingham were recently confirmed as the largest and busiest ports in the UK; 2003 figures show over 54 million tonnes of traffic.

The Labour Party MP for Grimsby, Austin Mitchell, is frequently in hot water with his party, as he staunchly upholds his independent views; he is determined to do his best for the town he has represented for 27 years. He is often at odds with party policy, and in 2004 he briefly changed his name by deed poll to Austin Haddock to publicise the difficulties facing Grimsby's fishing industry.

In 1769 there were eight alehouses in the borough, which equates to one alehouse to about every 100 inhabitants. Only two of the houses, the Wheatsheaf and the White Hart, now exist - the latter has been re-named O'Neill's Irish Pub. The Wheatsheaf is the oldest public house in Grimsby to still retain its original name.

THORNTON ABBEY 1893 33275

22

In the Civil War, Lindsey for the most part declared for the King, and the Royalist cause was warmly supported by the Earl of Lindsey, Viscount Newark, Sir Peregrine Bertie and the families of Dymoke, Heneage and Thorold.

GRIMSBY, PEOPLES PARK 1904 51832

Frank Brown, at one time proprietor of the Black Swan Inn, left to run an old blacksmith's shop and granary opposite. His wife, whose temper was not one of the sweetest, managed the inn. One of the customers, a rhymester, perpetrated the following:
'The children of Israel prayed for bread,
And God sent them manna;
Old Frank Brown prayed for a wife,
And the Devil sent him Hannah.'

The abundance of superlative freezing and packaging plants, the largest frozen storage capacity in Europe, and the logistical excellence of Grimsby's geographical position all help the town prosper. With houses priced 34% below the national average, the reduced cost of living is the envy of much of the country.

Nun's Corner was originally the site of St Leonard's Nunnery. Here, a small group of Benedictine nuns, established in the time of Henry I, were finally suppressed in 1543 by Henry VIII.

Ken Dodd, perennially young, never fails to sell a thousand seats with his annual pilgrimages to town, but be prepared if you go to one of his shows. It is quite normal to expect an after midnight finish, and he frequently doesn't leave the stage before almost one in the morning.

GRIMSBY, FISH PONTOON 1906 55750

GRIMSBY
A MISCELLANY

By 2003, Grimsby was officially Britain's luckiest lottery town, with eleven major wins in the area since the first draw in 1994. Individual wins of £14 million, £8 million and £3 million alone have helped earn Grimsby the nickname 'Winsby', and experts believe that the population of 110,000 is two-and-a-half times more likely to land a fortune than the rest of Britain.

GRIMSBY, THE DOCKS 1893 33272

During the Second World War there were 46 airfields in Lincolnshire. The local airfields, particularly Binbrook and Scampton, saw much action as Wellington and Lancaster bombers took off on nightly raids. It was from RAF Scampton that the famous 617 Squadron Dam Busters raid was launched in 1943.

In the 1970s many significant developments affected Grimsby, not least the infamous Icelandic cod wars. The Icelandic government imposed first a 50-mile and then a 200-mile exclusion zone around their country to protect fishing stocks and their own interests. This ruined a massive source of profit for Grimsby trawlermen. Gunboats were necessary to control the Icelandic waters as trawl lines were cut and shots were fired across the bows of trespassing UK trawlers.

The Bull Ring, as its name implies, was the place where the cruel sport of bull baiting was carried on – it was conducted under the official direction of the mayor. In later years the Bull Ring was enclosed with posts about three feet high with a top bar. Entrances were at each corner and midway on each side, except the narrow end to Bargate. In the centre of the enclosure stood a pump, and near it was the large stone to which the bull was chained in the days of bull baiting.

Some of the post-war salvage material from the demolition of the abandoned seaward part of Cleethorpes pier was used on Leicester City Football Club's new Filbert Street stand.

Oliver Cromwell himself came to Grimsby to ransack the home of Royalist supporter Gervase Holles in the 17th century.

GRIMSBY, BULL RING c1965 G60057a

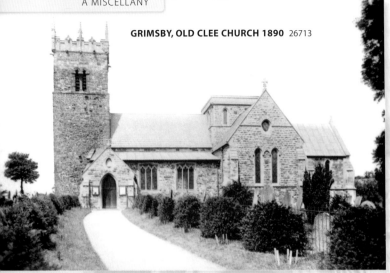

GRIMSBY, OLD CLEE CHURCH 1890 26713

Over the centuries, the surface level of the town has grown higher: the floors of old houses are below the level of the road. In digging the cellar of the house at the corner of Riby Street in 1863, some posts were found in a regular and upright position, whose tops were about seven feet below the surface of the road. In ancient times there was an inlet from the Humber at this point, and the posts, no doubt, were the supports of a landing stage.

In the 1830s the two main political parties here were the Whigs (the reds) and the Tories (the blues). When Lord Street was built, the residents were extremely staunch Whigs. This may have been from political conviction, or from the widespread bribery that went on at the time. This street, which ran from Flottergate to Cartergate, was known as Red Hill.

Did You Know?
GRIMSBY
A MISCELLANY

At the dawn of the Victorian age, Grimsby still suffered (as most towns did) from unhealthy and unsanitary conditions, poor personal hygiene habits, and the resultant inevitable disease. An outbreak of smallpox hit the town in 1830, and just two years later 246 people died as cholera arrived. The cholera epidemic was nationwide, and demonstrated the relationship between diseases and filthy unhygienic poorly-drained streets.

GRIMSBY, ROYAL HOTEL 1890 26724

GRIMSBY, CORN EXCHANGE AND MARKET PLACE
1890 26725

Traditional enmity between the north and south banks of the Humber estuary is part and parcel of Humber life. Grimsby and Hull compete for fish, after all! Thus when a genius in central government decreed that the South Riding of Yorkshire and North Lincolnshire would be combined into a single unitary authority of Humberside, it was a marriage made in Hell. In local government terms, 'Humberside' was abolished in April 1996.

GRIMSBY, ROYAL DOCK 1890 26722

The Grimsby Dock Tower, a 309ft-high building and arguably Grimsby's most famous landmark, was designed by James William Wild, who modelled it on the Torre del Mangia in the Palazzo Publico in Sienna, Italy.

The dock tower has for 150 years been a source of many fantastic stories. The first is that the foundations are built upon large bales of cotton to absorb water seepage from the river. Secondly, it is claimed that one million bricks were necessary to complete the construction of the tower. Finally, perhaps most bizarrely, it is claimed that the millionth brick is enclosed in a glass case.

When the foundations for the new Municipal Electricity Works in Moss Road were laid in 1899, the project, priced at £50,000, would provide 460 kilowatts of energy to power 60 streetlamps - but it only provided electricity for seven domestic users.

During the Second World War, it was feared that the pier presented an easy access point for seaborne invaders from Germany – they might be able to alight from ships or U-boats without entering inshore waters. Subsequently a middle section of the pier was removed, reducing the length of the part attached to land to just 355 feet. When the war ended, the Government were unable to fund a replacement, and so the isolated seaward section was demolished.

Grimsby produces more pizzas every day than Italy produces in a month, thanks to several massive production lines such as the Heinz San Marco frozen pizza plant.

The Royal Hotel (see photograph 26724 on page 31) was actually named the Royal Dock Hotel, and in a delightful architectural touch, the initial letters of the names of a series of carved stone animal heads situated above each of the ground floor windows spelt out Royal Dock Hotel. The building survived for 101 years until in 1966 it was cruelly demolished to make way for the existing railway flyover of the A180 at Lock Hill.

GRIMSBY, THE OLD MARKET PLACE c1965 G60102

**GRIMSBY, THE HAVELOK STONE OUTSIDE
THE WELHOLME GALLERIES 2004** G60702

The Wheatsheaf Inn stands on the corner of Welholme Road, where there used to be an old windmill, a post mill which ground corn - it burnt down around 1790. When the site was excavated shortly after, a bronze Roman eagle banner-head was found.

Locally made Tickler's jam was doubly useful in the First World War, for once the contents of the tins were consumed, the empty tins were refilled with explosives to make excellent hand grenades, which were known colloquially as 'Tickler's Artillery'.

GRIMSBY, CENOTAPH AT NUNS CORNER 2004 G60707

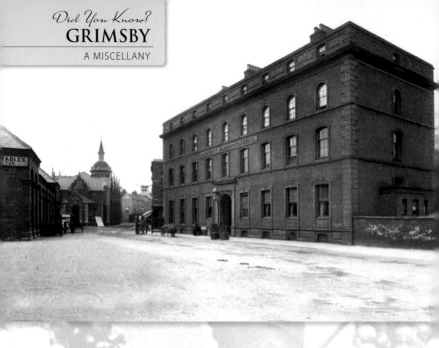

GRIMSBY, YARBOROUGH HOTEL 1890 26727

In former years Grimsby had three sets of stocks, two of which stood in the Bull Ring. They were used as a punishment for drunks and vagrants, and the Bull Ring stocks could admit two people simultaneously - both men and women could be punished in this way. The stocks were abolished by 1870. The last drunkard to be punished in the stocks was one Jack Mackinder; it was a cold and snowy day, and Mrs Emerson, a baker in the Bull Ring, kindly fed him a beefsteak pie dinner. For this exercise of charity, the then mayor decreed she would be prosecuted for supplying a prisoner with food, but no punishment was ever meted out.

The Yarborough Hotel (see left) has now been converted into a J D Wetherspoon's public house, voted Grimsby and Cleethorpes pub of the year several times by the Campaign for Real Ale. It remains a popular landmark in the town and retains its original name.

Conditions in the Town Hall gaol in Victorian times were far from pleasant. Gaol beds were straw with blankets, whilst leg-irons held troublesome prisoners. The gaoler could not allow 'spirituous liquors' in the gaol, nor suffer 'tippling or gaming'. Meals consisted of 'four penny-worth of bread per day, and one pound of coarse meat a week, except a prisoner for debt, who should not be sustained by, or have the allowance, on any pretence whatever, unless he pays for such himself.'

GRIMSBY, HOSPITAL 1890 26730

SPORTING GRIMSBY

Grimsby Town Football Club was formed during a meeting at the Wellington Arms public house in September 1878. The club was initially named Grimsby Pelham in honour of the Pelham family - Pelham was the family surname of the Earl of Yarborough, the most prominent landowner in the area at the time. After just one year, the club's name was changed to Grimsby Town. The club moved to its current home of Blundell Park after spells at Clee Park (1879-1889) and Abbey Park (1889-1899). The nickname of Grimsby Town FC is the Mariners.

The highest recorded attendance at Manchester United's Old Trafford football stadium is 76,962 - but not for a Manchester United match. Instead it was for the FA Cup semi final between Wolves and Grimsby Town on 25 March 1939. Unfortunately, the Mariners lost!

Former England national football team manager Graham Taylor was once the fullback for Grimsby Town. Injury forced his early retirement and a move into management at neighbouring Lincoln City.

For many years, a favourite quiz question in English football trivia was 'Which league football team play all their games away from home?'. The answer was of course Grimsby Town, whose home stadium of Blundell Park is in the neighbouring borough of Cleethorpes. These days this is no longer a unique situation, as several teams have shared a ground during the building of new stadiums.

The legendary Bill Shankley managed Grimsby Town in 1953. He went on to find fame as the manager of Liverpool in later years. One of his many memorable quotes is his comment on the off-side law: 'If a player is not interfering with play or seeking to gain an advantage, then he should be'.

Grimsby's sporting heroes include cross-channel record-breaking swimmer Brenda Fisher; the former British number one-ranked tennis star Shirley Bloomer, who married the athlete Chris Brasher; and the former top-ranked snooker players Mike Hallett and Dean Reynolds.

GRIMSBY, ST JAMES'S CHURCH 1893 33274

QUIZ QUESTIONS

Answers on page 50.

1. Whose statue stands outside the Associated British Ports offices beside Grimsby Docks?

2. What was the name of the maternity home at Mill Road, Cleethorpes, where many local people came into the world?

3. What is the connection between the site of Grimsby's Cenotaph and the hangman?

4. Which dock does the Corporation Bridge traverse?

5. What are the five carved figures outside Grimsby's public library known as? (They can be seen in photograph G60714 on page 9.)

6. Which king granted Grimsby its first charter, in 1201?

7. Which infamous building was built in 1802 and is now known as Albert Terrace?

8. Name the boy being carried on the shoulders of Grim the fisherman on the statue in the grounds of Grimsby College of Technology (see photograph G60703 opposite).

9. Which international festival is held on Cleethorpes Beach each year?

10. What was the original purpose of the Grimsby Dock Tower?

GRIMSBY, THE STATUE OF GRIM AT NUNS CORNER 2004 G60703

RECIPE

NORTH SEA FISHERMEN'S PIE

Ingredients

For the filling:

350ml/12 fl oz milk

1 bay leaf

Half an onion, finely sliced

450g/1 lb haddock or cod fillet

225g/8oz smoked haddock fillet

3 hard-boiled eggs, chopped

25g/1oz butter or margarine

25g/1oz plain flour

75g/3oz shelled prawns

2 tablespoonfuls chopped fresh parsley

Lemon juice to taste

For the topping:

500g /1¼ lb potatoes, cooked

40g/1½oz butter

60ml/ 4 tablespoonfuls milk

115g/4oz grated hard cheese of choice

Salt and pepper

Place the milk, the bay leaf and sliced onion in a saucepan over a medium heat and add the fish. Cover, and poach the fish lightly for 10 minutes. Strain, discard the bay leaf and reserve the milk for the sauce. Flake the fish into a buttered pie dish, discarding the skin and any remaining bones. Add the chopped eggs to the fish. Melt 25g/1oz butter in a saucepan on a low heat, stir in the flour and cook gently for 1 minute, stirring continually. Remove the pan from the heat and stir in the reserved milk that the fish was poached in, a little at a time and stirring continually so that no lumps are formed. When all the milk has been mixed in, return the pan to the heat and bring the mixture to the boil, stirring continually as the sauce thickens, then simmer the sauce for about 4 minutes, still stirring all the time. Remove from the heat and stir in the prawns. Add the parsley, lemon juice and seasoning to taste. Pour the sauce over the fish and eggs in the pie dish, and gently mix it all together.

To make the topping

Gently heat 40g/1½oz butter in 60ml/ 4 tablespoonfuls of milk in a small saucepan until the butter melts. Add the milk and melted butter to the cooked potatoes, mash and then beat until smooth. Spoon the mashed potato over the fish pie mixture to cover, and score the surface with a fork. Sprinkle the grated cheese over the pie before baking. Bake the pie in a pre-heated oven at 180°C/350°F/Gas Mark 4 for 25-30 minutes, until the top is golden.

RECIPE

LINCOLNSHIRE PLUM BREAD

'Plum' in recipes usually means dried fruit such as currants, raisins and sultanas, but in this recipe plums are indeed used, albeit in their dried form as prunes. This is especially good if the dried fruit is soaked overnight in cold (milkless) tea before cooking.

Ingredients

450g/1 lb plain flour (strong breadmaking flour is best)

225g/8oz prunes, cut into small pieces

115ml/4fl oz milk, warm

110g/4oz butter, melted

4 tablespoonfuls caster sugar

50g/2oz currants

50g/2oz sultanas

15g/ ½oz easy-blend dried yeast

2 eggs, lightly beaten

1 teaspoonful ground cinnamon

1 teaspoonful ground allspice

1 pinch of salt

Mix together the milk, sugar, butter, yeast, beaten egg, salt, and spices. Add the flour, and beat the mixture until it is smooth, to make soft pliable dough. Turn out the dough onto a floured surface, and knead it until it is smooth and elastic. Place the dough in a bowl, cover, and allow the bowl to stand in a warm place until the dough has doubled in size.

Knock back the dough and knead it again briefly, adding the dried fruit and making sure that it is evenly distributed. Divide the dough into two pieces, and place into two 450g (1 lb) greased and lined loaf tins. Cover and leave again in a warm place rise until doubled in size.

Pre-heat the oven to 190°C/375°F/Gas Mark 5.

Place the loaf tins on a pre-heated baking sheet and bake for 40-50 minutes, then remove the loaves from the tins and return them to the oven to cook for a further 5-10 minutes, or until they sound hollow when tapped on the base. Store the loaves in an airtight container and serve in slices, spread with butter.

GRIMSBY, THE DOCKS 1893 33273

QUIZ ANSWERS

Questions on page 44.

1. Prince Albert, husband of Queen Victoria (see photograph 26728 on page 20). Prince Albert laid the foundation stone of the new Royal Dock in 1852.

2. Croft Baker Maternity Home.

3. The Cenotaph is on the land once known as Gallows Hill.

4. The Alexandra Dock.

5. The Guardians of Knowledge.

6. King John.

7. The House of Industry, later called the Workhouse.

8. Havelok. 'The Lay of Havelok the Dane' tells how Havelok, the orphaned son of the King of Denmark, was cast adrift on the sea by his evil guardian. A raft bore the child to the coast of Lincolnshire where he was found by Grim, the legendary founder of Grimsby, who brought him up as his own son. When he grew up Havelok discovered the truth about his birth and returned to his homeland, eventually becoming King of Denmark. During his youth Havelok became renowned for his feats of strength. He once went to the court of Alsi, the King of Lindsey, at Lincoln, where he worked in the royal kitchens. King Alsi had promised his daughter Goldburga to the strongest and fairest man in the land. At a stone-throwing contest Havelok managed to lift one great stone higher and hurl it further than anyone else, and thus he won the hand of his wife. The Havelok Stone sits outside the Welholme Gallery in Grimsby, though whether this is the very stone reputedly thrown by Havelok to win the hand of Goldburga is for romantics to believe.

9. The International Kite Flying Festival.

10. To provide the massive head pressure of stored water necessary to operate the Royal Dock gates - these were necessary to harness the tidal ebb and flow of the Humber estuary. Latterly it provided a low-pressure water supply to the whole of Grimsby's extensive fish market.

GRIMSBY, THE DOCKS TIDAL BASIN c1955 G60009

GRIMSBY, MARKET PLACE c1955 G60015

FRANCIS FRITH

PIONEER VICTORIAN PHOTOGRAPHER

Francis Frith, founder of the world-famous photographic archive, was a complex and multi-talented man. A devout Quaker and a highly successful Victorian businessman, he was philosophical by nature and pioneering in outlook. By 1855 he had already established a wholesale grocery business in Liverpool, and sold it for the astonishing sum of £200,000, which is the equivalent today of over £15,000,000. Now in his thirties, and captivated by the new science of photography, Frith set out on a series of pioneering journeys up the Nile and to the Near East.

INTRIGUE AND EXPLORATION

He was the first photographer to venture beyond the sixth cataract of the Nile. Africa was still the mysterious 'Dark Continent', and Stanley and Livingstone's historic meeting was a decade into the future. The conditions for picture taking confound belief. He laboured for hours in his wicker dark-room in the sweltering heat of the desert, while the volatile chemicals fizzed dangerously in their trays. Back in London he exhibited his photographs and was 'rapturously cheered' by members of the Royal Society. His reputation as a photographer was made overnight.

VENTURE OF A LIFE-TIME

By the 1870s the railways had threaded their way across the country, and Bank Holidays and half-day Saturdays had been made obligatory by Act of Parliament. All of a sudden the working man and his family were able to enjoy days out, take holidays, and see a little more of the world.

With typical business acumen, Francis Frith foresaw that these new tourists would enjoy having souvenirs to commemorate their days out. For the next thirty years he travelled the country by train and by pony and trap, producing fine photographs of seaside resorts and beauty spots that were keenly bought by millions of Victorians. These prints were painstakingly pasted into family albums and pored over during the dark nights of winter, rekindling precious memories of summer excursions. Frith's studio was soon supplying retail shops all over the country, and by 1890 F Frith & Co had become the greatest specialist photographic publishing company in the world, with over 2,000 sales outlets, and pioneered the picture postcard.

FRANCIS FRITH'S LEGACY

Francis Frith had died in 1898 at his villa in Cannes, his great project still growing. By 1970 the archive he created contained over a third of a million pictures showing 7,000 British towns and villages.

Frith's legacy to us today is of immense significance and value, for the magnificent archive of evocative photographs he created provides a unique record of change in the cities, towns and villages throughout Britain over a century and more. Frith and his fellow studio photographers revisited locations many times down the years to update their views, compiling for us an enthralling and colourful pageant of British life and character.

We are fortunate that Frith was dedicated to recording the minutiae of everyday life. For it is this sheer wealth of visual data, the painstaking chronicle of changes in dress, transport, street layouts, buildings, housing and landscape that captivates us so much today, offering us a powerful link with the past and with the lives of our ancestors.

Computers have now made it possible for Frith's many thousands of images to be accessed almost instantly. The archive offers every one of us an opportunity to examine the places where we and our families have lived and worked down the years. Its images, depicting our shared past, are now bringing pleasure and enlightenment to millions around the world a century and more after his death.

For further information visit: www.francisfrith.com

INTERIOR DECORATION

Frith's photographs can be seen framed and as giant wall murals in thousands of pubs, restaurants, hotels, banks, retail stores and other public buildings throughout Britain. These provide interesting and attractive décor, generating strong local interest and acting as a powerful reminder of gentler days in our increasingly busy and frenetic world.

FRITH PRODUCTS

All Frith photographs are available as prints and posters in a variety of different sizes and styles. In the UK we also offer a range of other gift and stationery products illustrated with Frith photographs, although many of these are not available for delivery outside the UK – see our web site for more information on the products available for delivery in your country.

THE INTERNET

Over 100,000 photographs of Britain can be viewed and purchased on the Frith web site. The web site also includes memories and reminiscences contributed by our customers, who have personal knowledge of localities and of the people and properties depicted in Frith photographs. If you wish to learn more about a specific town or village you may find these reminiscences fascinating to browse. Why not add your own comments if you think they would be of interest to others? See **www.francisfrith.com**

PLEASE HELP US BRING FRITH'S PHOTOGRAPHS TO LIFE

Our authors do their best to recount the history of the places they write about. They give insights into how particular towns and villages developed, they describe the architecture of streets and buildings, and they discuss the lives of famous people who lived there. But however knowledgeable our authors are, the story they tell is necessarily incomplete.

Frith's photographs are so much more than plain historical documents. They are living proofs of the flow of human life down the generations. They show real people at real moments in history; and each of those people is the son or daughter of someone, the brother or sister, aunt or uncle, grandfather or grandmother of someone else. All of them lived, worked and played in the streets depicted in Frith's photographs.

We would be grateful if you would give us your insights into the places shown in our photographs: the streets and buildings, the shops, businesses and industries. Post your memories of life in those streets on the Frith website: what it was like growing up there, who ran the local shop and what shopping was like years ago; if your workplace is shown tell us about your working day and what the building is used for now. Read other visitors' memories and reconnect with your shared local history and heritage. With your help more and more Frith photographs can be brought to life, and vital memories preserved for posterity, and for the benefit of historians in the future.

Wherever possible, we will try to include some of your comments in future editions of our books. Moreover, if you spot errors in dates, titles or other facts, please let us know, because our archive records are not always completely accurate—they rely on 140 years of human endeavour and hand-compiled records. You can email us using the contact form on the website.

Thank you!

For further information, trade, or author enquiries
please contact us at the address below:

**The Francis Frith Collection, Oakley Business Park,
Wylye Road, Dinton, Wiltshire, England SP3 5EU**
Tel: +44 (0)1722 716 376 Fax: +44 (0)1722 716 881
e-mail: sales@francisfrith.co.uk **www.francisfrith.com**